Footnotes to Water

Zoë Skoulding

SEREN

Seren is the book imprint of
Poetry Wales Press Ltd.
57 Nolton Street, Bridgend, Wales, CF31 3AE
www.serenbooks.com
facebook.com/SerenBooks
twitter@SerenBooks

The right of Zoë Skoulding to be identified as
the author of this work has been asserted in accordance
with the Copyright, Designs and Patents Act, 1988.

© Zoë Skoulding, 2019.

ISBN: 978-1-78172-526-9
ebook: 978-1-78172-527-6
Kindle: 978-1-78172-528-3

A CIP record for this title is available from the British Library.

All rights reserved. No part of this publication may be reproduced,
stored in a retrieval system, or transmitted at any time or by any means,
electronic, mechanical, photocopying, recording or otherwise without
the prior permission of the copyright holder.

The publisher acknowledges the financial assistance of the Welsh Books Council.

Cover artwork: Ben Stammers

Author photograph: Anna Terék

Printed in Bembo by Latimer Trend & Company Ltd, Plymouth.

Footnotes to Water

Contents

FOOTNOTES TO WATER

Adda
  I   9
  II   10
  III   11
  IV   12
  V   13
  VI   14
  VII   15

Observation Chamber   16
Gull Song   17
Archaeology Report   18
Adda Rising   20
Miasma   21
Secret Reverse   22
What you thought   23
Trails   24
Hyacinthoides non-scripta   25
Haunt   26
Walking the Adda: A Collaboration   28
Maeyc's Pond   31

HEFT

  in the hoof   35
  how does a sheep   36
  people think   37
  look at you   38
  a gentle animal   39
  is this   40
  here we come   41
  at eye level   42

TEINT

  I   46
  II   47
  III   48

IV	49
V	50
VI	51
VII	52
VIII	53
IX	54
X	55
XI	56
XII	57
XIII	58
XIV	59
XV	60
XVI	61
XVII	62
XVIII	63
XIX	64
XX	65
Notes & Acknowledgements	66

FOOTNOTES TO WATER

Tarannon
   Terannon
       Tranan
           Toranon
                   Avon Dronwen
               Toronnen
                   Taran
                        Tarannis
                            Tarent
                        Trent
                    Trisantona
                        Afon Adda
           Afon Cachu

Adda

I

a river behind itself
this long *s* disappearing
seriffed into mud or the
torn edges of a map is

Adda or Adam after
Cae Mab Adda never
an origin only a
dried up rib of a river

a trickle of threat suppressed
escaping the level eye
where sea runs to horizons
innocent as water as

an adder stamped underground
with only the faintest hiss

II

river subtracted from its
own presence a river run
aground secretly working
as all rivers the double
edge of every beginning
blacked out in concrete pipes

where flood is defenceless where
water levels the difference

digging the foundations it's
as though no-one remembers
the water the ground is full
of it pumped out only to
rise up through the mud alive

III

flowering at the mouth it
speaks its own name on the point
of losing it becoming
public at a safe distance
our mouths flower in a name
becoming distant to us

what's vibrating underground
echoed in metal lids as
the town dips towards what it's
forgotten what's still there on
the tip of the tongue a rush
of kingcup campion bramble

in its stutter is what it's
saying what it's saying is

IV

the camera points at the
faces the river flicks out
of view trout between fingers
gone it was the faces we
held in the chemical frame
the soldiers the beautiful
grocer's daughter in shadow
moving through light the city's

dream of itself constructed
on water running under
unspeech in the dank edges
look away now the image
wet at the corners you would
never even glance at it

V

your fluency your vowels
your filth and your contagion
emerge from the mud and rock
becoming the system where
whatever hygienically
comes out of nothing the push
and pull of water under
ground that doesn't even know
how to speak its own language

in its solitude the beach
is a dead end not the way
out or was it ever land–
locked coffers sink and the slate
glitters like all that isn't

VI

doesn't everything run to
the lowest point your cut-price
sables budget peacock silks
flown all the way from China
an hour on the till the price
of a bus fare and the day
ends with all of us in it

river I ask you what is
the point where do you run to
how will you surface is it
only stoppage or sudden
mass that storms the pipes
into these puddles peacock
slicks rising on oiled weather

VII

what's the difference between a
form and a constraint does one
bottle up the other smash
the pattern by showing no
answer only the edges
where does the pressure come from
a crack in the shopfront or
here a spring coiled in a rock
displacement of energy
the shape of a stream inside
remaking itself into
this movement under soaked earth

spent-out water running through
where trickledown never did

Observation Chamber

what comes before a stop · is the swell of what
would run if · it could find a route to · the lowest
point · iron depressions count the way down ·
put an ear to the metal plate where · a river fizzes
through the pipes · a plotted course in rusting discs
or squares · that punctuate the distance scoring
where the level rises and falls · a work-shaped
hole that didn't ask to be · a question of a man ·
a woman welling up · the shape of a human
when the work stops · the men with nowhere
to go but · and the women with nowhere to go
but · water takes the quickest route · or gets caught
on the surface · dodging behind the drive-thru
where fashion turns over · the season always
cut price · are you listening · where no light falls
except · in pin-pricks on red water · black water
from the quarry · inaudible pressure · escaping

Gull Song

we come into the vacuum where the city was and we become
the vacuum you can hear your hunger speaking in our noise
and you can hear your hunger for the sea where you
came in like us and now we want your flat roof and your
sandwich we want the whole of the sea and the brooding clouds
our cries cut through your dropped ice cream and your almost
empty bag we come with necks like monuments to nothing
we come with eyes as cold as spreadsheets there is no warmth
in our endless whiteness just the grey shadow of possession
wherever you are you can hear us we came in with the herring
and stayed we came further in gathering your waste in our
plastic beaks we are rhythm distributed in space we're
stamping on the ground to make the rain come the worm rise
we see a hand move to a mouth we come closer you see us
we back off we live in your debt in the wreck of your greed
we scavenge in the turned tide of lunch we come nesting
who cares where we lay as long as there's a ledge or the
edge of a cathedral roof we are just too much and we live in
the too much of the takeaway the too many kebabs and chips
we dance with your too many leftovers we are leftovers too
with prehistoric feathers look at our eyes you are under
our surveillance our cries drown out your voices look at us
look at us hanging on look at us we almost love you

Archaeology Report

it starts with a wattle fence as a boundary
later a drain and wall are constructed
where nothing's left that's worth repeating
but a thick irregular piece of glass

both the drain and wall are constructed
over the line of a small ditch dated
by one thick irregular piece of glass
the base of a flask-type wine bottle

over the line of the small ditch dated
therefore as the earliest feature found
by the base of a flask-type wine bottle
worn away by intense wave action

which is therefore the earliest feature found
where all you can remember is the future
worn away by intense wave action
scattered belongings moving downstream

where all you can remember is the future
a pattern of ditches draining the gardens
our scattered belonging moving downstream
where all you can see in the water is yourself

a pattern of ditches draining the gardens
the things you wash away become your face
and what you can see in the water is yourself
fenced off in a name but flooding through

the things you throw away become your face
turned towards a stranger or a neighbour
fenced off in a name but flooding through
the edge of land that is just a beginning

turned towards a stranger or a neighbour
dysgwch am berygl llifogydd i chi
the edge of sea is just the beginning
of a movement repeating itself or breaking

dysgwch am berygl llifogydd i chi
it starts with a wattle fence as a boundary
a movement repeating itself until it breaks

Adda Rising

From 11pm on 18th Sept to 1 o'clock pm on the 19th we had rainfall of 1 3/4 inches which caused the Adda to overflow its banks. The water found its way across the Friars Fields to Orme Road and flooded Orme Road and Beach Road a depth of about 14 inches in parts and found its way into 78, 80 and 82 Orme Road...

– Borough Surveyor in report to Health Committee, Bangor City Council, 23rd October 1922.

Water seeps up the skirting board
and doubles the descending stairs
so they turn back
        and run under themselves.

You know that if you
        stepped into that reflection
certain laws would be suspended.

                The river
stretches into mottled walls,
        wicking up cracks in plaster
where the houses drink it in.

The darkness blisters like a thought –
paint it over.

The spume and froth is nearly nothing

but the skin of air and water
        where it swims and blurs,
                storming the gutters.

That hiss underground is the other
        side of the image.

Miasma

...look very carefully at all the house closets and pipes, and also to the street drains, and whether the sub-soil is dry and clean... This Bangor typhoid is so disastrous a thing.

– Florence Nightingale, *Letter to William Rathbone MP,* 1882.

the city sang the air the song was

    or its air sang us

we aired the song

  and sickness came out of the water

      like mist or muffled voices

rising from the marsh at night

     we never asked

who made the shape of the air

     or who owned it

  or why this place

   and not another

but we didn't trust the fog

     and the sickness unfolded in the air
a rumour

  in the stench of fetid water

and the river's hushed breath

     crept in the unaired

  unsunned room

     both body and murderer

Secret Reverse

Here the river isn't rain unscrolling
backwards from a mouth, a think
bubble waiting to fall, or a body

with underground senses, catching
the smell of emptiness, the taste
of invisible streets.

You search for the river while
the river searches gravity,
asking who knows and who
decides who knows: this
agitation under the surface.

Illegible data threads the contours,
river code written in the dark
where water holds no trace
of a pulse, a path, your eye
stopped on this pause –

What you thought

What you thought the buildings
were made of crumbles
in your hands. We fill our
mouths with two for the
price of one. There is Chinese
polyester hanging where the
words were where the purple
loosestrife was. There are gulls
filling their mouths where the
profit margin was. There are
three days of gathering clouds
and the cheapest is free. Just
out of reach is the water I can't
think or hear. A sudden
contraction further upstream
and the flow halts. There was stone
arched over voices where
the silence is. There's the name
of a river where the river was.

Trails

Slugs in the kettle spout. Trails across the floor
like miniature Styx. Lethe. Silver threads
in case they forget the way back. Silver links
like thinking. Damp surrounds us like death
in the musty chapels neat and flowered
bright and beautiful on Sundays. Jerusalem
Bethlehem Bethesda hot dry lands.

Hyacinthoides non-scripta

After R. Williams Parry's 'Clychau'r Gog'

They come with the cuckoo and go
when she's gone, paint the town
blue and stun it with wild scent.

Say hello and wave goodbye
under the trees unscripted,
a blue noise flowering in the cuckoo.

Silent bells arrive in the air, the grass
deeper than it was before, un-
documented feathers ringing blue.

Honeysuckle weight of a summer night –
hello, the nightingales are way off-course
in a blue song wavering goodbye.

The city migrates, rowing into
the sound of untranslated waves
and a blue excitable wind.

Haunt

The River Adda appears a thorough misfit in this structurally initiated valley, which was further widened and deepened by glacial meltwater at the close of the Pleistocene period.

– Peter Ellis Jones, 1986.

The city's made of interlocking habits and this is what makes it vanish. All you can see is what's out of the ordinary, but it's the unseen pattern that shifts beyond recognition. Underneath, the Adda reaches to its oceanic future, deep and glittering. In the car park on Caernarfon Road, everything's at a standstill between ENTRANCE and EXIT, under trees that started growing when the river ran in the open.

You can see where the rock was cut away to build the shops, the upper slopes covered in wire to stop falling stones or branches. If one day it might be difficult to read in this landscape the difference between the effects of the movement of ice or water and those of the flow of capital, they are, at this moment, not to be confused. A woman leaves a car, holding by the hand a small child in blue who is pointing at something invisible.

What feels like loss might be simply the pain of a broken habit, the anaesthetic of repetition wearing off. That is, the loss was already there and all you ever had was the repetition that covered it in a fine mesh of daily actions. A tall figure, leaning slightly sideways, has a box of plants under one arm. Others walk by slowly, wearing trainers and shorts. Not far away there is a gym, where people go to take care of their bodies through repeated movements, in the belief that such repetition will lead to a long and healthy life.

A boy in a baseball cap limps along to a red car where a girl is waiting with the bonnet up. He tries to touch something but jumps back as if it's too hot. Even though I'm not in their line of vision, they sense me watching and glance back. He closes the bonnet and they drive off. They disappear out of the picture and I'm already forgetting what they look like.

Ac eithrio / i ddanfon nwyddau. After 'Except', the bottom line, 'for deliveries,' has been crossed out with a wavy line of grey spray paint like a child's drawing of water. No way through except for the river. Everything's moving in the distance, or I am, as if behind glass, here where the water delivers itself in flood. Faces I can't see pass in cars, air full of traffic and seagulls. This is the pattern in which I have learned how to perceive and act.

Dandelions and self-heal are growing in the verge. Writing this made me look up the name of self-heal, which I didn't know, although I knew the plant from childhood, when I was closer to the ground. Cars pass. A repetition, not a repetition, an insistence. The trees in front of me are oak and beech. There are potholes in the road.

The river cuts a line of darkness that, from underneath, is pinpointed with light. *Why do things get in a muddle?* Your sense of how objects should be distributed in space rules out the possibility of the misfit river. There are infinite positions to be occupied, but only one that matches your idea of order in a landscape.

Haunting's no more than a pattern, a frequency – how a home is made. Or unmade. A sleeping bag unravels in the grass. The city digests the city, the valley expelling itself into the sea. Or the river's what escapes, leaving nothing but its tail. Everything's up for rent where signs mark the spot, over and over. You can't see the sea for the giant hoarding with its impossible surf.

Walking the Adda: A Collaboration

Text formed from comments made on and after public walks along the Adda in 2016.

It's here I understood 'watershed' for the first time. There used to be a pool here with two different kinds of fungus: black dimpled spheres and turkey tails. The whole place had to be refitted after the Christmas floods. If water is the eye of earth, sometimes it blinks. All you can hear above the traffic is seagulls. What happens to run-off? Are there fish in this river? Is it alive? It was in the fifties when my Taid fished for trout. There's a stink of river in the car park but we only think about it when it floods. All this water has to go somewhere. A willow tree in the car park points to water underground. What's under our feet? The river came into this shape like a body falling, or becomes a body of water only in falling to the lowest point. Here we used to gather watercress. At this point I had a real feeling of the old valley of Bangor with grass here and across the valley on the other side. The eye projecting light, shut. The mountain's cut away and that's why it floods. *Daeth y geiriau tlws yn flodau'r eithin.* We carry the silence of the water inside us. Does Bangor have a centre? Now it's Caernarfon Road – around the Cathedral is the Old Quarter. There's the flow of the river and then over it the flow of human behaviour – Saturday shopping, fast food, skatepark boys showing off, DIY, empty sodden parks. And here's the backstage – hidden gardens, sheds, fences rubbish. Decay and grey filth. Tell me tell me tell me tell me.

★

Crwydryn y ddinas yn cario'i gwastraff. Half way down the river you start to hear the flow of the water above the drain covers. I can feel the pull of the water here, tuning into it like radio. *I'r pant y rhed y dŵr.* How many times a day do you cross the Adda? A damp corner of the room, the creeping bloom across the wall, the opening crack: read the signs. *Mae llifogydd yn bygwth y tŷ hwn.* Water sleeps in every mirror. It pulses under our feet, beneath car tyres, beneath sheds. This was where the python disappeared for months and then turned up again on the doorstep as if nothing had happened. It must have gone underground, into the river where the rats were. This was where they collected pigeons' eggs. It's not the actual germs but an image of the river as pestilential vapour that leads to its disappearance. Some of these back streets I've never been down before. Forgotten water. You know the baby elephant in the Natural History Museum that came with the fair and died here? They rotted it down to its bones by putting it in a pond, and when they tested the water years later it was full of microbes that weren't from round here. Overlapping lives. The Old Glan of course used to be called The Three Salmons – you could see the sign when they did the renovations a few years back. Now we're in the Old Quarter. There used to be a pond with frogs in it – there's an eleventh century bridge in the Bible Garden. Here's an old brick wall I'd never noticed. You can hear it gurgle when it's raining – and when isn't it? Interior noise. Is it saying any more than the sound of the blood in my head? *Mae hi'n llafar yma.* A far more hollow sound.

★

When they were building the new shops the foundations kept flooding over and over. The ground was full of toxic sludge when the gas works was demolished, an acrid smell everywhere, coming through the windows of my office. And the workers digging it all up, red eyes behind goggles, sore throats. Going down to see what's there carries with it the fear of not being able to see it because it's what we are. It's still boggy underfoot in the football field alongside Ceiriog. The river was the boundary in the turf war between the kids of Garth and Hirael. As the rain falls, insurance goes up – but the river always lives at the bottom of the heap. Or the city's resting on a thin, shifting liquid that's invisible until it's gone: this is metaphor, not physics. In the reculverting, the chestnut avenue lost trees that have been replaced by oaks. When the pool was being built I rode a bike down the slope to the end full of mud: that's me, a six-year-old daredevil. A calculation of risks at the ocean's edge. Uncle Percy was trying to jump across the Afon Cachu with the other kids when he fell in. Pinning our hopes to level seas. I remember a foundry on Beach Road – that would be the tyre place now. I sneaked into the access hatch and dipped my toes into the Adda. Here was where Italian prisoners of war lived and made gardens outside their huts, one with a miniature leaning tower of Pisa, another with mosaics of blue and green sea glass. They'd smoke eels on the beach, dangled over a fire. Were there eels in the Adda? Always that sound of masts clinking in the wind when the old boatyard was there. Eleven thousand steps from Topps Tiles to the Crosville Club, *rhydd o'r diwedd, rhydd o'r diwedd, rhydd o'r diwedd.*

Maeyc's Pond

Interview with Maeyc Hewitt (1959–2015), March 2015, Caernarfon Road, Bangor.

I would get to an angle where I couldn't see the road. I was smaller of course but I was out of sight, and I was then in my own little world. Fantastic. It was a bit like a drainage ditch I suppose. And it was heavily grassed right up to the bank, so you couldn't exactly get to the bank because it didn't really exist. It was just grass, all wet and muddy, and then water, except for where the bridge was, where there were foundations, so there was a bit of hard ground. So it was like that on both sides and it formed a pond, sufficiently deep, say up to about here. I found out because I fell in. I was so fascinated I was going *what's that, what's that*, so I leaned in and put all my weight on one of the old railway sleepers and it just gave way, so I got a lot closer to the water than I was expecting. It had everything in it. Everything you'd find in the *Observer Book of Pond Life* was in this pond. It was absolutely pristine. There were two types of stickleback, three-spined and five-spined, making nests and everything; water scorpions; water boatmen; whirligig bugs; larvae; beetles; water-spiders – I was fascinated by them, even though I hated spiders I just couldn't – how on earth – it was fantastic. And also things I didn't even recognise. It was like a fish tank. Clear water, gently running, barely moving. And all this stuff living in it. I don't remember when I last saw a stickleback. They're fascinating because they build nests by gluing little grains of sand or rocky bits into a kind of tunnel. And they sit in this tunnel with their head sticking out of one end and their tail sticking out of the other. Just a little fish this long. Then it lays its eggs, and sits there, and protects the eggs. Absolutely amazing.

HEFT

in the hoof

in the hoof comes the heft
                or the drift of it
                              a slow word inching
by teeth marks over the hill
              a lifetime finding
                          the good grass the shelter
what wandering did we learn
              from the voice that pulls us back
                          all we like sheep
in the heft comes the weight of it
              pulling the wool over ownership
                          I know my own and my own know
nothing but this pattern repeated
              land knitted into bleating
                          graphs of profit and loss
in the drift is the learnt
              map of *cynefin*
                          meaning what you know is
moving in the same circles
              and what you know is
                          ownership eating the life
out of the slow hill
              the pattern repeating
                          and the word for it

how does a sheep

how does a sheep
                know where to go
                                molecular frisking in clouded sun
all the tuneless organs
                a shepherd's pipe
                          singing an embryo music
machine of sheep and human
                fleeced and plugged in
                          the eye's memory
remaking itself in darkness
                out in the mountain rain
                          browsing image after
image in chomped grass
                it's no longer certain who
                          I'm following or who
follows me in the huddled
                mass where I belong in that I'm
                          coming after the others
and before and alongside
                in the press of one body against
                          another not forgetting
the rasp of a bleat asking
                where are we going
                              the same unanswered question

people think

people think I could
                make another Dolly
                              but they don't understand
that there would never be
                another sheep like her
                              a copy of copies imprinted
I wanted so much
                to grow wild
                              branching out in
contradictory time zones
                where the hills were dead
                              it's all wrong but it's
all right at least I could run
                losing myself in disposable
                              bodies no longer animal
not yet machine
                common and close
                              neither dumb nor blonde
and turning back you glimpse
                a species receding in so many
                              versions you can't count
or failing the lookalike contest
                for being false enough
                              to seem completely real

look at you

look at you looking at me
                every which way
                              falling in pieces
steady the gaze
                steady the horizon
                              where we dance together
one head turning after
                another species a crossing
                              in the movement from here
to where the memory was
                grass flattened and
                              rising the spring of a stem
lifts the muscle
                tenses and the limb
                              shifts the landscape
that judders in the eye
                panning out sideways
                              in shallow patterns
kaleidoscopic shadow
                spooking the flock
                              that wanders beyond itself
a collective tremor
                multiplies in ears
                              travels twitching flanks

a gentle animal

a gentle animal
                its body clad in wool
                              harmless, placid by nature
but what you're counting
                every night what you dream
                              is electric an energy
passing through this
                body all wired up like everyone
                              zoom out on woolly maggots
or a tin turned upside-down
                the weight of it baaing
                              a buzz in the hand
alive as an insect
                trapped in dense wool
                              the tick and the flea
chewing through tomorrows
                that are eaten by yesterdays
                              for this read habitat
a fully automated system
                keeps ticking over
                              from red sky in the morning
to deserted glass blue hills
                that fade in circles
                              nibbled to the root

is this

is this what thinking is
            this browsing the tips
                      a constant rumination
where we wander
            at the back of the brain
                      in impossible forests
in the trace of a movement
            with wired primrose eyes
                      you never noticed
in a zig-zag movement
            of multiplied inheritance
                      running sideways
or looping to infinity
            a figure of eight
                      repeating the day's journey
in the silences between
            the words stretched out
                      in a Möbius strip
where you can't tell
            which way the landscape
                      will unfold itself next
we sniff the grass
            grip it the head moving
                      swiftly forwards and up

here we come

here we come flocking
                defaid undivided as
                              fluffy atoms massing
where a thought becomes
                contraction of muscle
                              hoof prints in wet grass
as we come through cloud
                glimpsed through heather
                              in sheep's clothing
where the wolves have gone
                this hock or pastern
                              could be mine or hers
or his or theirs or anyone's
                the sky held up by
                              multiple blue screens
tipped at an angle
                where only the lost ewe
                              wanders sheepishly
or trots full pelt
                into the sodden landscape
                              watched by a hollow socket
shrinking to a speck
                or a tangle of wool
                              caught on the wire

at eye level

at eye level what comes
                running towards you
                              in a broken movement
as the sky jumps
                the grass goes out of
                              focus where your own bones
face another in relations
                that stop nowhere
                              under the skin
of a voice a broken
                moment coming back
                              bydd yn ôl but it's never
byth yn ôl to the same
                place some place
                              almost the same
where almost is drizzle
                and most is mist
                              coming down over
the pastures where
                the past is leading you
                              beside the still pool
reeling back death in
                digital flicker through its
                              shadows and valleys

TEINT

Teint

for the Bièvre

The Bièvre today represents the most perfect symbol of feminine misery exploited by a large city. [...] Like many country girls, the Bièvre fell prey, upon her arrival in Paris, to the industrial snares of touts; despoiled of her dresses of grass and adornments of trees, she had to set to work immediately and wear herself out with the terrible chores demanded of her. Surrounded by rough merchants who pass her daily, but, by common agreement, imprison her in turn the length of her banks, she has become a tannery worker, and, day and night, she washes the filth from stripped skins, soaks the spare fleeces and raw leather, suffers the grip of alum, the bite of lime and caustic. There you see her in the evenings behind Gobelins, in a foul-smelling sludge, alone, trampling in the mud, by moonlight, crying, dazed with fatigue, under the miniscule arch of a little bridge.

J.K. Huysmans, *La Bièvre*, 1914.

I

Not a river but its
                shadow harmonics hidden
level in the glass note
                      glissando between a
movement and a sound
                        half in the performance
where I ran to you I
                ran as tainted water

while tarmac shines in rain
                        the channels you don't touch
well up on tomorrow's
                    tongue to flower there don't
leave or was it this way
                    that now I'll run from you

II

    Not a trace but the same
                              line writing itself
over and over again
                        it can't wash away
the evidence that
                        gathers in the silt or
in the edges of a
                        map of the city's growth rings

a habitat constitutes
                        the physical structure
perceived by living things
                        each living thing
also a habitat the human
                        becoming river

The uninhabitable: sea as rubbish dump, coasts bristling with barbed wire, bare ground, mass burial ground, heaps of carcasses, boggy rivers, stinking towns

– Georges Perec, *Species of Spaces*, 1974.

III

Not a beginning but
                       backwash hidden upstream
industrial blood scrubbed
                            clean away chopped offal
the skins you didn't see
                     stitched into the polis
rinsed into leather boots
                         for wars fought in footsteps

if blood hangs in sight lines
                         reddening the mirrors
look away as water
                 swallows every story
the city's vibrating
                   skin behind it more skins

IV

    Not drowning but buried
                            the lost body always
    hers always innocent
                  already filthy her
    live arm absent from dead
                        arm lifting hydraulic
    weight to feed the mills
                    diverted into sewers

    this slow disappearance
                  into age a reason
    to sink in concrete what
                    you can't face you never
    could only call back in
                  song to the safely dead

V

Not wormwood but stream of
                                piss so says Rabelais
six thousand and fourteen
                                dogs went howling after
the woman in crimson
                                Panurge couldn't charm so
his revenge a river
                                of dog-desire maddened

by scent the dogs all came
                                at once they pissed on her
they pissed at her door in
                                streams of bitter water
this territory marked her
                                satin asking for it

Panurge had no sooner spoke this but all the dogs that were in the church came running to this lady with the smell of the drugs that he had strewed upon her, both small and great, big and little, all came, laying out their member, smelling to her, and pissing everywhere upon her – it was the greatest villlainy in the world. […] When she was entered into the house and had shut the door upon herself, all the dogs came running of half a league round, and did so well bepiss the gate of her house that there they made a stream with their urine wherein a duck might very well have swimmed, and it is this same current that now runs at St Victor, in which Gobelin dyeth scarlet, for the specifical virtue of these piss-dogs […].

– François Rabelais, *Gargantua and Pantagruel* II Chap. XXII, 1534, trans. Thomas Urquhart and Peter Anthony Motteux 1693.

VI

Not a torrent but furred
                        mud silks through time stopped up
to flood a future where
                  beavers have vanished with
only *bièvre* to bite
                its way into the tongue
castoreum musky
            your sillage at arm's length

dog-river bares its teeth
                at the devil's dye-house
this quality of water
              mordant how do you like
my scarlet what will this
                will it never be clean

VII

Not a river but its
                      nymph already complaining
late 1500s in
              Baïf's lament for injured
water where your goblins
                        where your poisons tint
inhuman dyers taint
                the mixing of our waters

her own name blotted out
                        by *Gobelins* she runs
in the glint of bare life
                are you even listening
the city doesn't
            count what lies underneath

VIII

Not the source but the effluent
                                    will rather the multitudinous
waves incarnadine
                making the green one
Gobelin scarlet
                  affluent in muddy commerce
all the insect blood of America
                              rinsed in the piss-poor river

runs as weft in this repeated
                          gesture where evenness
is all that hangs
                between hand and eye
a landscape opens on a wall
                      the wool pulled over

IX

Not a rill but run-off
                          guttering to a halt
or flood that stutters in its
                                struggle with silence
you have to be so quick
                            to catch the impossible
when money falters time
                          sells out the cuts cut in

her wavelength takes you down
                                her flame red her curlicue
stepped in the bitmap weave
                              that makes it seem natural
on the rue Berbier-du-Mets
                              in steeped scarlet the slow loom

X

Not black ribbon but white
                              silences deserted
streets a bleached dust under
                                    August moon cool ermine
traced with silver thread
                              shivers under scraped skins
say snow of leather or
                       city drowned in feathers

you can't get far enough away
                                  to see the glacial picturesque
without the ripped hide
                           stench and bloodstains
seeping into utterance
                               between the river and itself

XI

    Not a vein but the lateral
                             piercing of boulevard
    Auguste Blanqui driven
                             underground it has become
    its own double the universe
                             yammering on while
    far away the sister
                             stars look back at us

    tangling and untangling
                             the endless alternatives
    of self by side by self
                             where revolution runs
    into hidden patterns
                             a cracked face a future

Nature neither knows nor practises morality in action. What she does, she does accidentally. She plays at blind man's bluff, destroys, creates, transforms. The rest don't notice her. With eyes shut, she applies the calculation of probabilities better than all the mathematicians can explain with their eyes wide open. Not a variant escapes her, not a chance is left at the bottom of the ballot-box. She draws all the numbers.

– Louis Auguste Blanqui, *Eternity through the stars*, 1872.

XII

Not a thread but a gut
                strung along arrondissements
where the feeling is
                microbial love that passes
understanding in our
                blue gentian candida
streptococcus waterlily
                phage from everywhere at once

why this is Paris in the
                weather repeating itself
nor are we out of it
                nor am I out of you
from secret to secretion
                as water undoes us

The underground tunnels, organs of the large city, would function like those of the human body, without revealing themselves; pure, fresh water, light and heat would circulate there like the various fluids whose movement and upkeep sustain life. Secretions would act mysteriously there, maintaining public health without troubling the good order of the town and without spoiling its external beauty.

– Georges-Eugène Haussmann, *Memoir on the Waters of Paris*, 1854.

XIII

Not a stream but a laundry
                          where the washer girls are
wringing and beating and
                      thumping the linen
rain running down their necks
                            to the arch of the back
no longer smelling of
                    amber and benzoin says Huysmans

the air that chokes them is
                    fecal bass notes overture
of soap to animalic
              accord a memory
in the dry-down of moss
                    earth harsh on the skin

XIV

Not oblivion but
                      a smudged line an oozing
cut across atmospheres
                          never to be erased
have you forgotten your
                            need for water does it
rise to stain the back of
                        your throat and are your lips

the borders of damp air
                        sifting through a passage
on the rue de Croulebarbe
                            tongue curling around the
dessication of letters
                    are you with me now

XV

    Not a *dérive* but
                    a double course looping
    back on itself where one
                          runs and the other turns
    aside until its weight
                    is all that carries it
    through its long to-do list
                          in the glittering sludge

    how do I get to the
                   other side you're on it
    already as much as
                 you'll never be the one
    arriving the second
                   the other doesn't leave

XVI

Not a conscious movement
                              but not without reason
he's just forgotten why
                      he's made the detour
through teasel and ragwort
                          Rousseau botanising
on the Bièvre avoiding
                      a boy who knew his name

water streams out of its
                        classification dodges
and weaves round old duties
                            remembered by no-one
begin with pimpernel
                      chervil borage groundsel

We have hardly any mechanical movement whose cause is not to be found in the heart, if we are acquainted with the manner of seeking it.

– Jean-Jacques Rousseau, 'Sixth Walk', *The Reveries of the Solitary Walker*, 1782, trans. Charles E. Butterworth, 1783.

XVII

Not memory but moire
                         in the silkstream's marbled
lines wet layers pressed on
                         cloth shifted like ray trace
or a photograph of
                         television before
it existed before
                         the river changed to this

bee hanging in breeze sus-
                         pended water's version
of itself held in a
                         breath doubling up as speech
behind Paris seething
                         its lava of events

The stream of silk and moire

−Victor Hugo, 'Bièvre', 1831.

XVIII

Not water now but ink
                          the river's leaking black
staining my hand in this
                              blotting out of image
its refusal to be
                      anything but body
touching its own absence
                                blind in concrete channels

curved and folded a
                    skin tattooed with its own
mottled pulse a tremor
                          sloughed off running in the
hollows all its water
                      pure evaporation

Is it mud or water?
Is it soot or ink?

– Claude Le Petit, *The Scandalous Chronicle or Ridiculous Paris,* 1668.

XIX

Not flooded marsh but ice
                            with skaters engraving
continuous serifs
                on the halted water
hacked white slabs a buried
                              meaning held till summer
cold in the mouth as speech
                            or the memory of it

what I'm selling you is
                            sepia standstill print
unlike the slow creak
                      of water vanishing
under its name a score
                        of the city's movement

XX

Not channel but wave form
                                      in this arrangement still
looping from the mouth and back
                                                  streaming all ears balance
tipped in its own labyrinth
                              how do you even say that
when voice accumulates
                          every river's accent

children yelling in a
                        cul de sac you can't go
back to where you came from
                                  it already floods you
echoes over high walls
                            rain pooling on tarmac

Notes & Acknowledgements

Footnotes to Water

These poems were written as part of *rAdda*, a collaboration with the visual artist Ben Stammers that explored the route of the Adda, the river that runs through Bangor but which has been entirely culverted for many years. Its name has the *dd* of Welsh, pronounced 'th' as in 'the'. It is also remembered locally as Afon Cachu – Shit River. A performance of the poems with Ben Stammers' photographs and sound by Alan Holmes can be found at bangoradda.org, along with further details of the project, which was supported by Bangor University's ESRC IAA fund and the Arts Council of Wales.

Archaeology Report uses text from the Gwynedd Archaeological Trust's *Historic Towns Survey of Gwynedd: Bangor*, Report No. 681 (2007) as well as an enquiry report produced by Angharad Stockwell. The phrase *dysgwch am berygl llifogydd i chi*, 'learn about your flood risk', is drawn from the Natural Resources Wales website.

Miasma: Florence Nightingale's letters to William Rathbone MP on the Bangor typhoid epidemic are held by Bangor University Archives and available online at www.peoplescollection.wales/items/7608. The poem also quotes from her 'Notes on Nursing: What It Is and What It Is Not' (1859).

Haunt: The epigraph is from Peter Ellis Jones, *Bangor 1883–1983: A Study in Municipal Government* (University of Wales Press, 1986). 'Why do things get in a muddle?' is a question posed and answered by Gregory Bateson in *Steps to an Ecology of Mind* (University of Chicago Press, 1972).

Walking the Adda: A Collaboration is composed of texts gathered during several public walks in 2016 co-curated with Ben Stammers, with contributions from Wanda Zyborska, Sarah Andrews, Scott Saunders, Rhiannon Little, Eleri Wynne Jones, G.M. Jones, Siân Melangell Dafydd, Shaun, Carolyn, Dylan, Alia and Seren Burkey, Elizabeth Woodcock, Rob Mimpriss, Lynne Heidi Stumpe, Lesley Conran, Alys Conran, Brigitte Kloareg, Irene Walls, W. Jones, Jane Kenney, Mel Williams, Jeremy Yates, Pam Green, Anna Powell, Jim Conway, Meryl Sebon, Huw Jones, and other members of the public who did not wish to be named – many thanks to them all.

Daeth y geiriau tlws yn flodau'r eithin. The beautiful words became gorse flowers.
Crwydryn y ddinas yn cario'i gwastraff. The city's wanderer carrying its waste.
I'r pant y rhed y dŵr. Water always flows to the valley (an idiom meaning that the rich always seem to get richer).
Mae llifogydd yn bygwth y tŷ hwn. This house is threatened by flooding.
Mae hi'n llafar yma. It's vocal here.
Rhydd o'r diwedd. Free at last.

Heft

These poems were commissioned by Miranda Whall for the multimedia project *Crossed Paths*, supported by the Arts Council of Wales, and were part of her exhibition in Oriel Davies, Newtown in 2018. Italicised lines in English are from Ian Wilmut, quoted in Sarah Franklin, *Dolly Mixtures: The Remaking of Genealogy* (Duke University Press, 2007), and 'Of the Sheep', Aberdeen Bestiary 20v-21r, Aberdeen University Library MS 24 (http://www.abdn.ac.uk/bestiary/ms24/f20v). *Cynefin* is Welsh for 'heft', localised knowledge passed on through generations of sheep, though used more widely to mean 'habitat'. Other italicised phrases in Welsh, *bydd yn ôl* and *byth yn ôl*, 'will be back' and 'never back', are from a dream. *Defaid*: sheep.

Teint

This sequence was written during a residency at the Centre International des Récollets, Paris, co-hosted by the Institut Français and the Mairie de Paris. Many thanks to Marie-louise Chapelle, Siân Melangell Dafydd, Chrystel Dozias, Alan Holmes, Nelly George-Picot, Jean Portante, Lionel Ray, Sarah Riggs and Fanny Rolland. I would especially like to thank Sioned Puw Rowlands, who first introduced me to the Bièvre, which until the early twentieth century ran through Paris between the 5th and 13th arrondissements. A performance of the text at the Maison de la Poésie in Paris, with music by Cathy Heyden and Alan Holmes, can be found at bangoradda.org.

Teint: For the Bièvre was previously published with Jean Portante's translation into French as a Boiled String/Hafan Books chapbook in 2016. Part of it appears in *Atlantic Drift: An Anthology of Poetry and Poetics*, edited by James Byrne and Robert Sheppard (Arc Publications/Edge Hill University Press, 2017).

Poems from this collection have also appeared in *Shearsman, Blackbox Manifold, Poetry Wales* and *The Fortnightly Review*. My thanks to the editors.